Just for Me!
Stories to Personalize

Joshua, David, the Good Samaritan, and Me

Visit Tyndale's exciting Web site at www.tyndale.com

Copyright © 2002 Educational Publishing Concepts, Inc., Wheaton, IL 60189.
All Rights Reserved.

Exclusive distribution by Tyndale House Publishers, Inc. PO Box 80 Wheaton, IL 60189
Produced by Educational Publishing Concepts.

ISBN 0-8423-6981-3

Printed in China.

08 07 06 05 04 03 02
7   6   5   4   3   2   1

JUST for Me! ™
Stories to Personalize

Joshua, David, the Good Samaritan, and Me

TYNDALE KiDS

Tyndale House Publishers, Inc.
Wheaton Illinois

STICKER 1

STICKER 2

STICKER 4

Mom continued, "The Israelite army was camped near Jericho. God had promised that they would capture Jericho. But when they got there, they found out there were big walls around the city. How were they supposed to get in? Joshua wasn't surprised to hear that God had a plan.

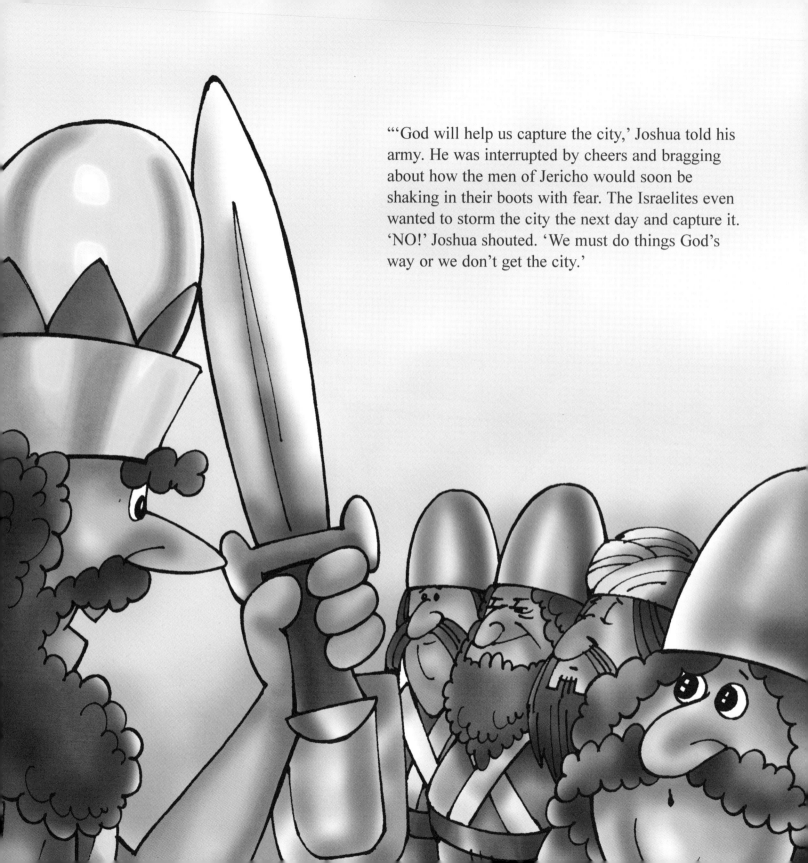

"'God will help us capture the city,' Joshua told his army. He was interrupted by cheers and bragging about how the men of Jericho would soon be shaking in their boots with fear. The Israelites even wanted to storm the city the next day and capture it. 'NO!' Joshua shouted. 'We must do things God's way or we don't get the city.'

"'We are to march around the city once a day for six days—in complete silence!' Joshua ordered. 'The seventh day we will march around seven times. Then we'll shout, and the walls of Jericho will fall down.' He must have been convincing because they did exactly what he said. The Israelites didn't make a peep, even when the men of Jericho made fun of them.

STICKER 6

STICKER 7

STICKER 9

"You know . . . David and Goliath. The story where the little guy stands up to the big giant and wins! Goliath was the big creep who made fun of God and King Saul's army, and David was just a little boy. He wasn't afraid of Goliath, even though all the soldiers were scaredy-cats. David wanted to stop Goliath from making fun of God.

"He asked King Saul to let him fight the giant. At first the king said, 'No, you're just a kid. Goliath has been a soldier longer than you've been alive.' But finally the king gave in. 'At least wear my armor,' he said. 'It will protect you a little.' David tried it on, but it was so heavy that he couldn't walk. 'Get me out of this. I have to do this my own way!' he shouted.

"King Saul's soldiers were amazed when David marched down the hill. Goliath couldn't believe it. He got steaming mad when he saw a kid coming to fight him. 'Come on, Kid, I'll feed you to the birds!' he shouted. 'I'm not scared of you,' David shouted back. 'You've got a big sword and shield to fight with. But I've got something even better! God is helping me!'

"David put a stone in his slingshot and swung it around over his head. When he let go, the stone flew toward Goliath. Everything seemed to happen in slow motion. As the stone hit Goliath's forehead, the giant wobbled and crashed to the ground. David won! The little guy won! Of course, he knew that he won because God was helping him.

STICKER 12

STICKER 13

STICKER 16

STICKER 18

"The story of the Good Samaritan reminds us to be nice to all people." Mom continued, "A man was on his way to Jericho. He walked along, enjoying the sunny day. Then some robbers jumped out, beat him up, and stole his money. They even took his clothes before leaving him beside the road. The man thought for sure he was going to die there. Then he saw a priest coming—surely a priest would help him. But he didn't. He just crossed the road and kept on going.

"Later, a temple worker came by. He saw the poor bleeding man, too. But he didn't help him either. Next a man from Samaria came by. His people and the Jews hated each other. He didn't even have to think about it, though. He stopped and helped the hurt man. He bandaged the man's wounds and took him to an inn. He made sure the man got good care and he paid for everything.

"The hurt man must have been surprised that it was a Samaritan who helped him instead of the church workers. When Jesus told this story, he said that we should treat others the way the Samaritan did. Does this give you any ideas?" Mom asked.

"The hurt man must have been surprised that it was a Samaritan who helped him instead of the church workers. When Jesus told this story, he said that we should treat others the way the Samaritan did. Does this give you any ideas?" Mom asked.

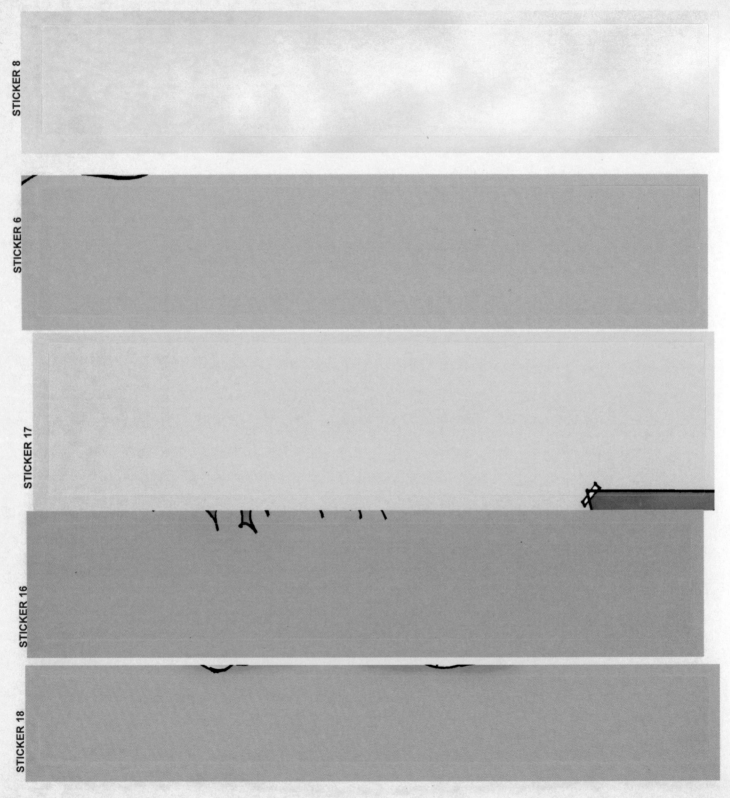

STICKER 8

STICKER 6

STICKER 17

STICKER 16

STICKER 18